THE
BRIGADE in REVIEW

THE
BRIGADE IN REVIEW

A Year at the U.S. Naval Academy

ROBERT STEWART

With a Foreword by
Vice Admiral William P. Lawrence, USN (Ret.)

NAVAL INSTITUTE PRESS
Annapolis, Maryland

Photographs and text copyright © 1993 by Robert Stewart

All rights reserved. No part of this book may be reproduced without written permission from the publisher.

Library of Congress Cataloging-in-Publication Data

Stewart, Robert, 1949–

The brigade in review: a year at the U.S. Naval Academy/Robert Stewart;

with a foreword by William P. Lawrence.

p. cm.

ISBN 1-55750-776-7 (acid-free)

I. United States Naval Academy.   I. Title

V415.L1S74 1993

359'.0071'173—dc20   93-1407

All names, logos, and symbols attributed to the United States Naval Academy in this book are trademarks

of the Academy and have been reproduced with permission of the United States Naval Academy.

Printed in the United States of America on acid-free paper ♾

3 5 7 9 8 6 4 2

First printing

This book is dedicated to Ensign John Mark Reimann, U.S. Navy,
of the U.S. Naval Academy Class of 1992
for his tireless enthusiasm, ideas, and intellect, which helped me to
learn how midshipmen survey their lives and futures.
From the first time I met John in May 1991 and the year that followed,
I saw how the personal qualities that made him a model Naval Academy midshipman
respected by his classmates in the brigade were certain to help him serve
with distinction as a naval officer.

FOREWORD

To fully appreciate the program at the U.S. Naval Academy, which Robert Stewart, the author and photographer, portrays so well in this excellent pictorial narrative, it is essential to understand what its graduates are expected to do in their military careers.

Our armed forces are charged with maintaining the nation's security, which sometimes requires that they engage in warfare with our enemies. The renowned General Douglas MacArthur, U.S. Army, expressed this eloquently to West Point cadets in 1962: "Your mission remains fixed, determined, inviolable—it is to win our wars . . . all other purposes will find others for their accomplishment, but you are the ones who are trained to fight; yours is the profession of arms."

Under our Constitution, military officers are expected to willingly subordinate themselves to civilian authority, one that can order them into situations where their lives are placed at great risk. Still, there has never been a serious challenge to civilian authority by the U.S. armed forces in the history of our country, a unique situation among the world's nations.

Military officers must always place America's interests and the welfare and safety of their subordinates above their own. They must meet these extraordinary expectations and highest standards, personally and professionally, in peacetime as well as war. It is imperative that the Naval Academy prepare midshipmen for the special roles they will fill when they are commissioned as Navy and Marine Corps officers.

A competent military officer, too, must possess a broad range of qualities, expressed so well by Captain John Paul Jones, father of the U.S. Navy, more than two hundred years ago: "It is by no means enough that an officer of the Navy be a capable mariner. He should be as well a gentleman of liberal education, refined manners, punctilious courtesy, and the nicest sense of personal honor." If Jones were living today, he would have used "lady or gentleman" in his statement because women now are an integral part of our armed forces and are well represented in our service academies.

Of all the qualities the Naval Academy imparts to its midshipmen, the two most essential are moral and physical courage, the sine qua non of the military officer. The Academy's program assigns preeminence to moral development. Every midshipman must live by the Honor Concept, which states simply that "midshipmen will not lie, cheat, or steal." Honor and integrity are attributes essential to military effectiveness, which is vitally dependent on strong mutual trust and respect among members of a combat unit.

Physical courage is the ability to perform difficult, demanding tasks often involving the risk of one's life. Midshipmen develop this quality in a regimen that requires twenty-four–hour accountability in every aspect of their performance and personal behavior.

Equal emphasis is given to academics at the Naval Academy. The chiefly technical yet well-balanced baccalaureate program ranks among those of the finest universities in our country. Academy graduates must possess a strong intellectual foundation. The responsibilities they carry out during their military careers are diverse and significant and often involve the highest affairs of state. The pyramidal rank structure of our military officer corps permits less than 50 percent of Academy graduates to serve for a full career. However, many pursue distinguished careers in other forms of public service and in the business world. In effect, the Naval Academy's rigorous selection process and intensive whole-person development program turns its graduates into genuine national assets.

Mr. Stewart's perceptive union of images and words clearly shows us that despite the unrelenting demands on midshipmen during their Academy days, they are typical, wholesome young people who enjoy the diverse extracurricular activities the institution provides, such as dances, movies, sports events, and musical activities. In an environment of serious commitment, midshipmen must, and do, find time to laugh and have fun.

With his superb book, Robert Stewart has rendered a fine service. His readers will understand and appreciate the challenging task of preparing young persons to fulfill in the military profession the noblest obligation that can be vested in the citizen of a nation, the protection of his or her country's freedoms and way of life.

Vice Admiral William P. Lawrence, USN (Ret.)
U.S. Naval Academy Class of 1951 and
Superintendent of the Naval Academy, 1978–1981

Admiral Lawrence graduated with distinction from the U.S. Naval Academy. As a midshipman, he wrote the Academy's Honor Concept. He was the first naval aviator to fly twice the speed of sound. During his second combat deployment in Vietnam, Admiral Lawrence was shot down and held as a prisoner of war for six years; he was awarded the Distinguished Service Medal for his leadership of fellow prisoners. The admiral's executive assignments included Assistant Deputy Chief of Naval Operations (Air Warfare), Commander, U.S. Third Fleet, and Chief of Naval Personnel. Since retiring in 1986, Admiral Lawrence holds the Chair of Naval Leadership at the Naval Academy.

INTRODUCTION

I first visited the U.S. Naval Academy in Annapolis, Maryland, in 1961 when I was thirteen years old. At the time, I thought more about the impressive size of Bancroft Hall, the dormitory building, and the special feeling of standing in Tecumseh Court, the ceremonial courtyard in front of the dorm, than about attending someday as a midshipman.

Thirty years later I visited Annapolis and the Naval Academy again. My purpose was to produce a photo documentary–style book representing one year in the life of the Brigade of Midshipmen. As I photographed and talked to midshipmen, Navy and Marine Corps officers, and Academy graduates, I regretted not having applied for a nomination and appointment to the Academy when I was young.

The time I spent there—sixteen months to work on this book—made a penetrating impression on me, as a photojournalist, as an outsider, and as an American.

With my cameras and lenses in tow, I was greeted with enormous interest and cooperation by the Academy's administrative staff and especially by the midshipmen. The "mids" are shamelessly proud of their institution, even occasionally arrogant. Because the Naval Academy is the central part of each midshipman's formative life, the superintendent's staff granted me wide passage to witness events there as they actually happen. From the everyday to the ceremonial, from broad smiles to braced chins, I quickly grew to understand why the Academy is a unique institution and why the midshipmen can love or hate it as they do. On balance, though, they are admittedly honored to be part of the Naval Academy and admire it for its treasures as well as tolerate its miseries. From one photo shoot to the next, I realized that they would not trade places with any other college-age peer in America. Perhaps the graduates' well-known saying appropriately describes life at the Naval Academy: "It's a tough place to be but a great place to be from."

This same broad exposure I had to the daily rhythms of Naval Academy life was valuable for me as an outsider. Many times I saw visitors, tourists, and midshipmen's parents or other family members standing in Tecumseh Court with curious expressions etched on their faces. They really wanted to walk beyond the cavernous and beautiful rotunda of Bancroft Hall and up onto the floors, or decks, of this huge, almost mysterious dormitory where the midshipmen live. To go inside and follow the sounds of an upperclassman shouting an order or the loud chorus of retorts from a platoon of plebes. They could not, but I could. Each journey I took on the decks of Bancroft Hall, down Stribling Walk with marching midshipmen, behind Mitscher Hall with a platoon of plebes on Induction Day, along the combat course during Leatherneck training at the Marine Corps base in Quantico, and inside King Hall as 4,200 midshipmen ate their meals was an education and a privilege.

The Naval Academy is much more than impressive formal parades of young men and women marching onto Worden Field with taut military bearing. It is a place where future Navy ensigns and Marine Corps second lieutenants learn several significant truths about life in and out of the military. Self-control and discipline are solutions to fear and chaos. Teamwork is essential, and confidence is invaluable. Pride is sturdy, and so is humility. Talk is sometimes cheap, but deeds are enduring. And diligence is a virtue of personal character, not a flaw.

Virtually every visit to the Naval Academy left me feeling confident as an American about the hands in which the national defense would be entrusted in the near future and beyond. I became very partial to the midshipmen as my association with them and their institution grew. I still am. The midshipmen I met and talked to, some of whom I developed close friendships with, uniformly possessed several personal qualities that I believe exist in every one of the young men and women who are there: They are confident, sometimes brash and cocky. Yet they have an impressive measure of humility and poise. You feel it when you are in their presence. Midshipmen are highly articulate and have a secure conviction about what they want to do with their lives. They can laugh at themselves as fast as they can snap to attention with deference at a Navy or Marine Corps officer's question or command. Each midshipman I met left me reassured that the Naval Academy ably prepares its young men and women faster and probably better than civilian universities do for the challenges and demands they can expect to encounter as adults.

Undergraduate life for midshipmen certainly includes commonplace routines and difficulties that perplex all college students. Some classes are exceptionally stimulating, some are rigorous, and at least one always seems to be boring. Social functions for meeting other college students are exciting and also anxious times—that is, simply normal. Expectations are high, though, even more self-imposed at Navy because midshipmen come to the Academy already intensely motivated. Midshipmen seem to pursue everything they do with a fervent determination to succeed. A "can do" attitude is pervasive, a staple of their way of life. The highly competitive application process that every plebe candidate goes through for an appointment to the Naval Academy is partly designed to reveal such perseverance. Approximately one of every twelve candidates, chosen from among many of the country's finest college prospects, are admitted to Navy. A few years ago, a candidate who was not selected showed up at the Academy on Induction Day. He told officials that he was certain at least one appointee would not come that morning, and he was there to fill that spot. He was convinced, he said, that he would succeed as a member of the brigade. That's the kind of determination midshipmen tend to possess.

Sixteen months spent with the Academy's administrators and midshipmen made me feel special as an adopted member of the Navy family but also taught me that this fine service academy and its uncommon environment are, above all, a choice that those who go to Navy must make themselves.

I enjoyed my days and nights among the Brigade of Midshipmen. The Naval Academy staff members I worked closely with are an outstanding team. Finally, I had the good luck to be at the Academy and to know its unique residents, observe its special traditions, and learn its rich history.

ROBERT STEWART

UNITED STATES NAVAL ACADEMY

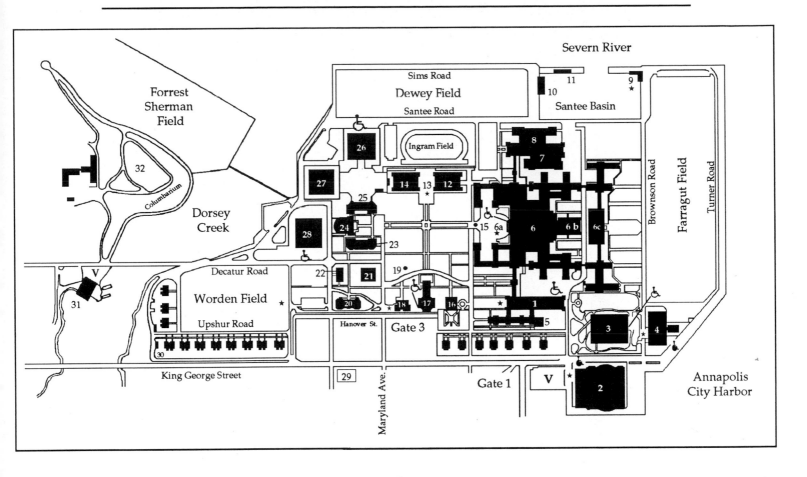

1. Dahlgren Hall
2. Halsey Field House
3. Lejeune Hall
4. Ricketts Hall
   (Visitors' Center
   Senior Enlisted Barracks)
5. Ward Hall
6. Bancroft Hall
   6a. Rotunda and Memorial Hall
   6b. King Hall
   6c. Mitscher Hall
   (Chaplain's Center, Inter-faith
   Chapel and Auditorium)
7. Macdonough Hall
8. Luce Hall
9. Robert Crown Sailing Center
10. Vandergrift Cutter Shed
11. Hendrix Oceanography Lab
12. Chauvenet Hall

13. Radford Terrace
14. Michelson Hall
15. Tecumseh
16. Buchanan House
    (Superintendent's Quarters)
17. Chapel
18. Administration Building
19. Herndon Monument
20. Officers' & Faculty Club
21. Preble Hall
    (Naval Academy Museum
    and Naval Institute)
22. Leahy Hall
    (Candidate Guidance Office)
23. Sampson Hall
24. Mahan Hall
25. Maury Hall
26. Rickover Hall
27. Nimitz Library

28. Alumni Hall
29. Alumni House
30. Officers' Housing
31. Hubbard Hall
32. Naval Academy Cemetery
    (Columbarium)
33. Public Safety Building

Lost & Found: Gate 3

★ Rest Rooms

♿ Rest Rooms With Facilities for
   Handicapped

♿ Entrance for Handicapped

V Visitor Parking

ANNAPOLIS, MARYLAND

I

PLEBE SUMMER,
FOURTH-CLASS YEAR

"Plebe Summer is the initiation to the initiation,
a preamble to plebe year. You cannot be a plebe without it."
Ronald H. Reimann, USNA '61

Each incoming class of recently appointed undergraduate students to the U.S. Naval Academy, called "plebes," traditionally starts its naval service in the first week of July.

Plebes officially begin their freshman, or fourth-class, year on "I" or Induction Day. The Class of 1996 was represented by 1,245 high school graduates, including enlisted personnel from the U.S. Navy and U.S. Marine Corps, selected for a Naval Academy appointment from 12,265 candidates who applied. At 6:00 A.M. the doors to Alumni Hall, also known as the Brigade Activities Center, open. The new Naval Academy appointees, many of whom lined up on the sidewalk even earlier, enter the building and say good-bye to parents, family members, and close friends until they see them again at approximately 6:30 P.M., when the new Naval Academy plebe class is sworn into the U.S. Navy by the Commandant of Midshipmen.

Once inside Alumni Hall, plebes check in, pick up name and baggage tags, fill out many forms, have their vision screened and blood drawn, and receive other preliminary medical checks. Next, they are given their first military haircuts. After leaving the barbershop, plebes receive their first issue of uniforms. The garments are regulation Naval Academy clothing that they will wear throughout Plebe Summer: athletic shorts, shirts, and tennis shoes. They are fitted for Plebe Summer "dixie cup" hats. And they each pack and carry a large laundry bag containing other uniform items, such as their "white works," the standard uniform that they will wear for their swearing in and for the majority of daily nonphysical training events throughout Plebe Summer's six intense weeks.

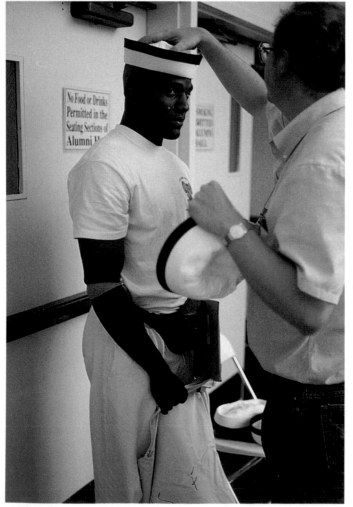

"Plebe year is an extremely uncomfortable prod that constantly forces you to reach your limit. But then you learn an important lesson: you set your own limits."

Christopher A. Eckerle, USNA '92

Minutes before the plebes leave Alumni Hall late in the morning on "I" Day for extensive medical and dental examinations, upperclass midshipmen assigned to the Academy for part of Plebe Summer instruct them on how to properly wear their hats (called "covers") by measuring the correct distance between nose and hat with two fingers, stand at attention and "at ease," and salute all upperclassmen and active-duty U.S. military officers. Then members of the new plebe class file out of Alumni Hall, toss their laundry bags into a truck, and depart by bus for Bancroft Hall, where they will pick up their gear after the noon meal. Bancroft Hall, or "Mother B" as midshipmen call it, is the enormous dormitory that houses all of the approximately 4,200 members of the Brigade of Midshipmen. This vast structure is the center of life for all midshipmen while they are on the Yard, the name for the Naval Academy's 338-acre campus in Annapolis, Maryland.

In the afternoon, both inside Bancroft Hall and in its adjacent courtyards, plebes meet their first-class midshipman platoon and company commanders and second-class midshipman squad leaders, who will guide the 108 squads of plebes (there are 36 platoons, each with 3 squads). These midshipmen are nominated for their duty assignments, known as billets, by their active-duty Navy and Marine Corps company officers, all of whom are top-notch officers, and are selected because they are considered models of naval leadership.

In the early evening family members and friends of the newest Naval Academy plebe class gather just inside the walls of Tecumseh Court to watch the Oath of Office Ceremony.

"Plebe year is the biggest slice of humble pie anyone could digest.
You learn from day one—the slate's clean, prove yourself."

Angela M. Smith, USNA '83

Marching in formation through Bancroft Hall's two arches that lead into T-Court, as Tecumseh Court is known to midshipmen, the plebe class fills the rows of chairs, standing at attention with eyes straight ahead and waiting for the platoon commander's order of "Seats!" After the Superintendent of the Naval Academy, a rear admiral in rank, welcomes the new midshipmen and their guests, the plebes are called to attention and are administered the Oath of Office: "Do you, . . . , having been appointed a midshipman in the United States Navy, solemnly swear that you will support and defend the Constitution of the United States against all enemies, foreign and domestic; that you will bear true faith and allegiance to the same; that you take this obligation freely and without any mental reservations or purpose of evasion; and that you will well and faithfully discharge the duties of the office on which you are about to enter, so help you God?" With their rights hands raised, the plebes answer, "I do."

Moments after the ceremony ends, plebes meet their families along the tree-shaded grass on Stribling Walk, the main sidewalk that runs through the middle of the ceremonial part of the Yard, for thirty minutes before they assemble back inside Bancroft Hall with their platoon commanders. Traditionally, this temporary "so long" before parents see their sons and daughters six weeks later at Plebe Summer Parents' Weekend in mid-August is a mixture of smiles, congratulations, and even tears. Plebes, parents, and friends alike understand that, good and bad, Plebe Summer will be an experience no plebe will ever forget.

"Plebe Summer is fast paced and challenging. Within ten to fifteen minutes, you will have run up the stairs from PEP, taken a shower, put on a fresh uniform, learned the menus for the morning, noon, and evening meals, wiped your cover, shined your shoes, read three newspaper articles, and still have made it to morning quarters formation three minutes early."

Grace S. Gee, USNA '93

The physical-fitness schedule designed for Plebe Summer is rigorous. Physical readiness, intended to develop a plebe's self-discipline and self-confidence simultaneously, is a core component of every midshipman's total program while at the Academy.

Plebes gather every weekday morning at 6:00 A.M. for PEP—Physical Excellence Program. Since 1968 plebes have filled Farragut Field, near the seawall at the rear of Bancroft Hall, to follow the exercise commands of Heinz Lenz, one of the Naval Academy's professors of physical education. During the forty-five–minute fitness regimen, the platoon commanders and squad leaders walk through the rows of exercising plebes to correct a technique, compliment a good effort, and shout encouragements. Physical fitness and organized athletic training constitute almost 20 percent of Plebe Summer. After PEP, plebes return to Bancroft Hall and have approximately twenty minutes to wash up, change clothes, and assemble in their squads before marching to the morning meal.

Squad leaders also guide their plebes through the specially designed obstacle course on Hospital Point field, which is separated from the rest of the Yard by Dorsey Creek. Each station presents a different objective for a group of approximately 5–7 plebes, simulating a situation in which leadership and teamwork are essential to completing the mission. Plebes receive direction and feedback from their squad leaders before, during, and after they work on each course station.

Seamanship and navigation instruction, shipboard damage control, flag signals, Morse code, and weapons training are subjects that occupy a large portion of a typical Plebe Summer day, which starts with reveille at 5:30 A.M. and ends with taps at 10:00 P.M. Other areas of study and training include close-order drill, swimming instruction, instructional sessions with squad leaders about Academy and naval-service traditions, lectures on the characteristics that a good officer needs to develop, intramural-sports competition, and personal time.

Plebes learn basic sailing skills in Rainbow-class knockabouts, or twenty-four–foot long boats, and later sail Laser dinghies and forty-four–foot sloops. The sailing program is aimed at teaching plebes boat-handling and sailing techniques, water-safety practices, and crew coordination.

"The Class of 1991 was ingenious for training the plebes. One time many plebes had to pass through the 'International Rate Line' to get to their companies. A large piece of decorated tape marked the Line. You felt like you were going through Customs. Every day was something new, and it combined what the upperclassmen dreamed up and how the plebes responded based on their tolerance to stress that day."

Christopher S. Beaufait, USNA '93

The pistol range at the Naval Station, which is located across the Severn River from the Yard, is where plebes learn and practice small-arms fire and marksmanship with .45-caliber semiautomatic pistols. Upperclass midshipmen and Marine Corps instructors teach the plebes about weapons safety, sight alignment, and trigger control. Nearby at the rifle range, plebes are taught the same important marksmanship practices with M-16 automatic rifles, known as "pieces." The purpose of this training is not so much to have midshipmen become expert marksmen, although the ability to shoot well will certainly be important to those who choose to enter the Marine Corps upon graduation, but to teach the plebes respect for safety rules and discipline in handling dangerous weapons.

Plebe dixie cups, marksmanship-training manuals, water canteens, Navy baseball caps, and a copy of *Reef Points*, a plebe's most important book, are left on the ground near the pistol range. A plebe must carry the pocket-sized edition of *Reef Points* wherever he or she goes. It contains encyclopedic information on naval seamanship and navigation procedures, Academy regulations, the Midshipman Honor Concept, and hundreds of other details germane to Academy life. Because Annapolis is very humid and hot in the summer, plebes need the water in their canteens to refresh themselves when they are marching on the drill field or working on the obstacle course, for example. The upperclassmen are responsible for keeping their plebe charges as healthy as possible and will cut back on physical activities if the weather gets brutal.

Upperclass midshipmen may stop plebes at almost any time of the day or evening on the Yard during Plebe Summer and on through the fourth-class academic year and order them, on immediate notice, to recite from a wide list of facts or "rates." Rates may include passages from *Reef Points*, the menu for the next meal, the names of the brigade officers of the watch, at least three news events or sports stories from that day's newspapers, and even special events scheduled that day on the Yard.

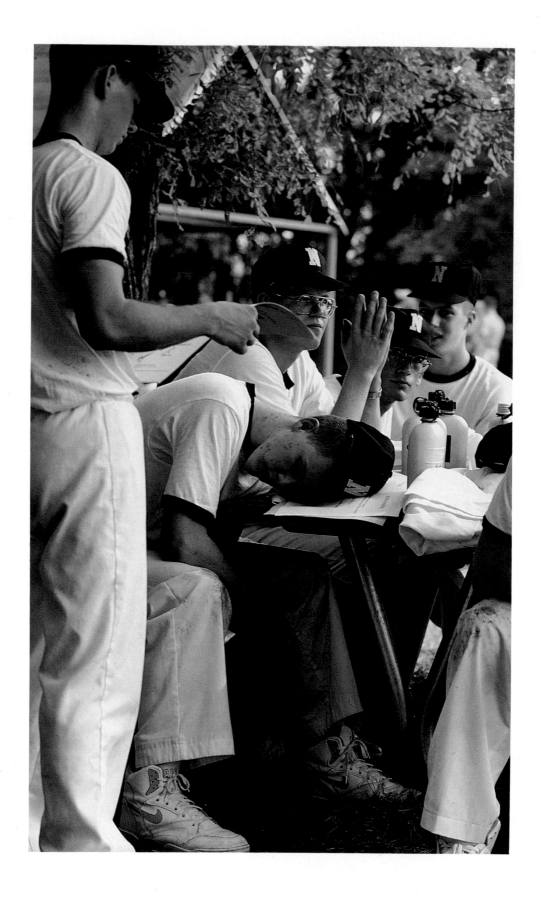

Plebe Summer is a relentless agenda of Naval Academy and naval-service indoctrination and education. Fatigue is every plebe's constant companion. Rest is a precious commodity, whenever a plebe can grab it for just a few moments.

Two plebes stand at rigid attention or "braced up" while a second-class midshipman (two diagonal gold stripes running across his shoulder boards) dictates the rules that control the plebes' behavior in King Hall, the name of the midshipmen's dining room.

For example, to get permission to ask a question, a plebe must first stick out his or her closed fist. He or she must also remember that a plebe always keeps his or her eyes "in the boat," that is, focused straight ahead. No "chipping," or casual conversation, is allowed among plebes while they are in King Hall.

During Plebe Summer, plebes must march into the 65,000-square-foot dining room. They must remain standing behind their chairs until the pre-meal announcements are finished and all upperclassmen—squad leaders, platoon commanders, and company commanders—as well as any active-duty military officers or civilian guests are seated. After placing their covers under their chairs, plebes must pass food to their squad leader, seated at one end of the table, and these others before they can serve themselves. Only after these senior-ranking persons have filled their plates and glasses can all the plebes serve themselves. Plebes must return their hands to their laps after every bite of food. From the time they enter King Hall until they march out of it, plebes answer an endless stream of questions and recite a bewildering number of rates ordered by upperclassmen, their intention being to teach the plebes how to think and respond coherently under pressure.

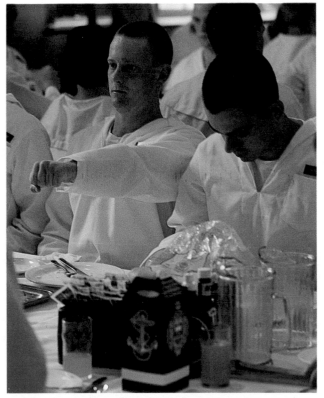

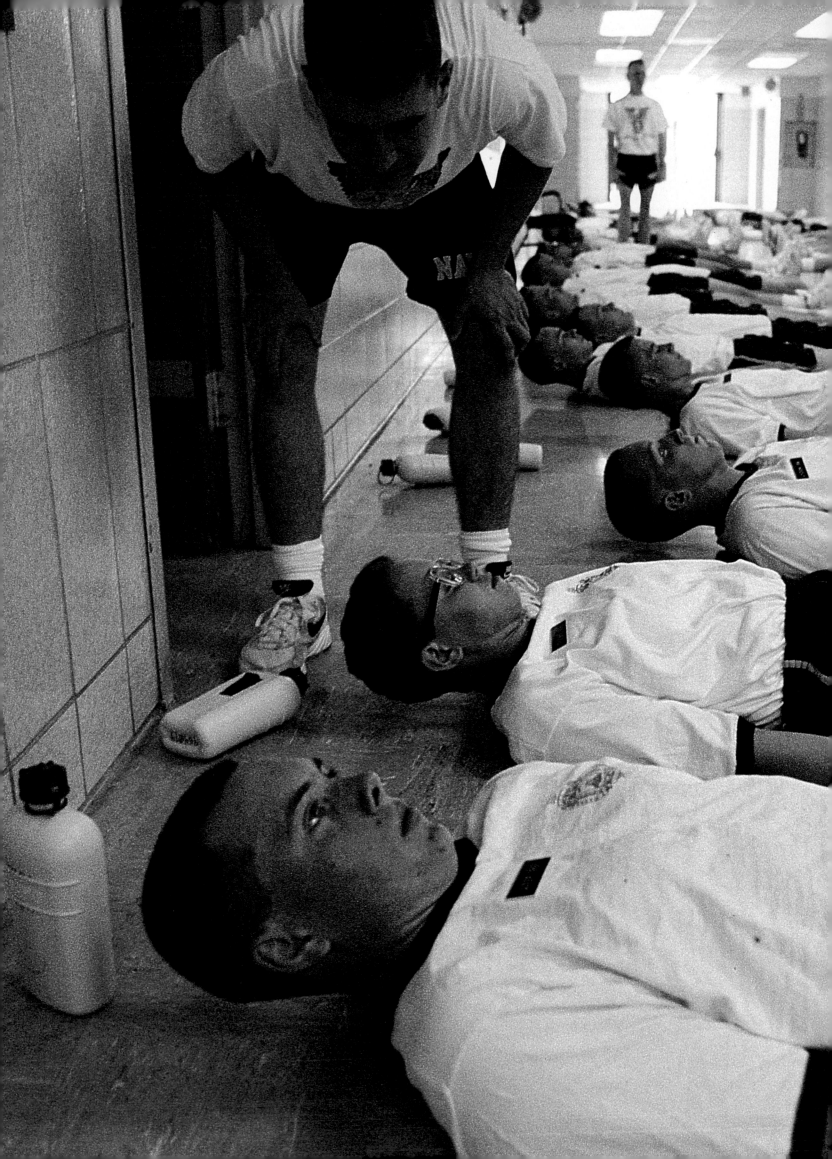

"During Plebe Summer, a member of my company couldn't help the constant five-o'clock shadow he had, despite shaving several times a day to get rid of it. A squad leader ordered him to sound off with 'Ya Ba Da Ba Doo, sir!' instead of the 'Beat Army, sir!' or 'Go Navy, sir!' that the rest of us used. His shadowy look reminded upperclassmen of Fred Flintstone, and they weren't going to let this plebe forget it."

John P. Fitzgerald, USNA '92

Squad leaders work with their plebes on the decks of Bancroft Hall as well as outside on the Yard. Sometimes the upperclassmen will emphasize physical conditioning. Other times, however, they will pose a rapid series of questions, expecting fast answers and also trying to instill in the plebes the ability to stay clear-headed under pressure, an ability that will be vital to their success as military officers. Plebes do not enjoy these sessions. Squad leaders and platoon commanders also spend time introducing the elements of military command and leadership, linking the physical exercise and mental pressure with self-confidence and the desire to lead others, even fellow plebes.

On Plebe Summer's Parents' Weekend in mid-August, the new plebe class finally applies hours of practicing close-order drill and presents to parents, friends, and the general public its first official parade on Worden Field as fourth-class midshipmen of the Naval Academy (without the rest of the brigade, which is still away for summer training). The weekend marks the first time families have seen their plebes since Induction Day in July.

After all thirty-six companies of plebes have marched onto the field, the colors are presented before an upperclass Plebe Summer officer and also the Superintendent of the Naval Academy and the Commandant of Midshipmen. Plebes stand at "present arms" with their rifles tightly held inches away from their chests. Finally, the Naval Academy band plays as the plebes pass in review before the superintendent and commandant.

"I'll never forget the starched cotton smell of thirty-six sets of fresh white works, while standing in morning formation during Plebe Summer. It's a smell all its own."

Robert L. Burgard, Jr., USNA '85

When the rest of the brigade returns to the Academy in late August, plebes learn that Plebe Summer was merely the start to a demanding fourth-class year. When answering a question posed by a senior-ranking midshipman, plebes are limited by custom and regulation to five answers: "Yes, sir. No, ma'am. Aye, aye, sir. I'll find out, ma'am. No excuse, sir." This restriction is more loosely governed now than in past years. Nonetheless, the return of the brigade is still menacing for a plebe. The plebe pictured here listens to an upperclassman at 6:55 A.M., shortly after the bells announcing reveille have sounded. At the end of the deck, another plebe stands silently at attention. In King Hall, one squad leader stops to question three plebes left at their table by another squad leader after the noon meal has ended.

At any time on the decks of Bancroft Hall, plebes will snap to an upperclassman's order for "chow call" or "come around," two of various compulsory features of the first and formative year of a Naval Academy midshipman.

Plebes are required to give "chow calls" ten and five minutes before every scheduled formation, which is when all midshipmen line up for inspections and announcements. These ten- and five-minute warnings tell the upperclassmen which uniforms are required for formation as well as the menu for the next meal, the schedule of upcoming events on the Yard, and other pertinent information. During chow calls, upperclassmen will often stand directly in front of the plebes, trying to trip them up in their recitations by making noise and causing other distractions. Such upperclassmen become known as "flamers" because they are seen as being out to get or "burn" their plebes.

This would be a typical chow call:

> Sir, you now have ten minutes until morning quarters formation. Formation goes inside. The uniform for morning quarters formation is winter working blues.
>
> The menu for morning meal is orange juice, assorted cereal, fresh fruit, pancakes with margarine/maple syrup, sausage links, bagels with cream cheese, coffee, milk.
>
> The officers of the watch are: Command Duty Officer is Lieutenant Ritz, United States Navy, 9th Company Officer. The Officer of the Watch is Midshipman Lieutenant Commander Rosen, Fifth Battalion Commander.
>
> The professional topic of the week is the Gulf War. The major events on the Yard are: 1100 Blood Drive Deck 5-0; 1500 baseball vs. Georgetown at Bishop Stadium; 1530 practice parade at Worden Field; 1900 Forrestal Lecture in Alumni Hall.
>
> You now have ten minutes, sir.

Plebes ordered to appear at an upperclassman's room at a specified time to take oral quizzes on military knowledge and current events are engaged in a "come around."

During the weekday from reveille until taps, plebes must move throughout Bancroft at a jogging pace—called "chopping"—and "square the corners" every time they make a turn into a room or down a corridor, which in Navy parlance is called a passageway. Plebes quickly learn that prior to entering the Navy they were calling many ordinary things by the wrong names. The floor is really a deck; the ceiling is an overhead; walls are bulkheads; stairs are ladders. These are the terms used aboard Navy ships, and the upperclass flamers are quick to correct any use of civilian language among the plebes.

The plebes on the preceding page have arrived at a come around and are reciting facts about U.S., allied, and other military jet aircraft to a first classman. When the plebes become third classmen, called "youngsters," and start their sophomore year, they will call the new plebes to come arounds.

"*Be sure to enter plebe year with a sense of humor.
Your first obstacle at the Naval Academy is usually yourself.*"

Timothy J. Reimann, USNA '87

II

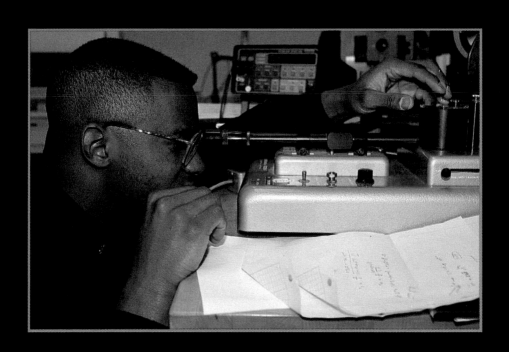

LIFE AT THE
NAVAL ACADEMY

*"The most important lesson I learned at the Naval Academy was leadership.
Not only was I taught the principles of leadership, but I was given an
opportunity to practice them and my performance was evaluated.
My business success is based squarely on applying those leadership principles
and maintaining the high standards taught at the Naval Academy."*

Ross Perot, Chairman, Perot Systems Corporation, USNA '53

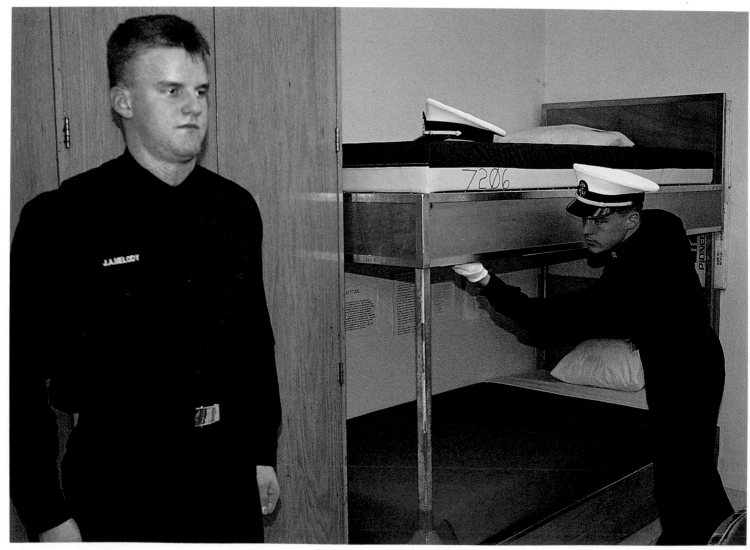

The decks of Bancroft Hall are silent from taps at 11 P.M. until reveille at 6:30 A.M. the next morning when bells ring throughout the building. Bancroft Hall, believed to be the second-largest dormitory of its kind in the world, is home to the entire Brigade of Midshipmen. It has 1,873 midshipman rooms, almost 5 miles of corridors, and approximately 33 acres of floor space.

Midshipmen live two, three, and sometimes four to a room. Their rooms are expected to be ready for walk-through inspections at all times during the day and must pass formal white-glove inspections several times each year. Between taps and reveille, though, upperclassmen do not live or sleep any differently from their counterparts at civilian colleges, except perhaps to stay up later to study.

Before the morning meal at 7:15 A.M., squads assemble on Bancroft Hall's decks, and squad leaders announce important messages to the midshipmen in their charge. These announcements generally cover any special activities the company will participate in that day, within or outside of the Yard.

The brigade is organized into two regiments, with six battalions in each regiment and six companies of approximately 120–25 midshipmen per company in each battalion. Midshipmen identify themselves by their companies. They eat meals, participate in intramural sports, often study, and sometimes even go on liberty, or leave, together.

Each company is made up of three platoons, each of which in turn is composed of three squads. A squad is twelve midshipmen. The squad leaders and platoon commanders are expected to provide leadership and counsel to any squad or platoon member who, at some point, has problems with academics, the Academy's strict environment, other midshipmen, or personal matters. The active-duty Marine Corps and Navy officers assigned as company officers do not intervene in any midshipman's problems unless that mid has first spoken with his or her midshipman chain of command, except in special, serious cases. An official staff of Academy academic counselors assists any midshipmen who have difficulties with course work. Each battalion also has a senior enlisted advisor—a Navy master chief petty officer or Marine Corps sergeant major—who can call upon their many years of service experience to counsel midshipmen.

Sometimes the squad leader's responsibility is difficult. A plebe may survive plebe year. After returning to the Yard after third-class summer training, the new third classman may still have difficulties adjusting to Academy and Navy ways. The squad leader's job is to help the new youngster fit in.

The Academy's administrators know that being a squad leader is a tough job. Even so, it is the kind of situation that prepares midshipmen for future command situations, in which officers or enlisted personnel under their command may face personal problems that would affect others in the unit.

After morning meal, the brigade empties out of Bancroft Hall's front entrances, walks across Tecumseh Court, and goes on to the first class of the day, saluting military officers on the way. Regulation dress for mids attending daily classes is working blues, and they must wear their covers any time they are outdoors. Those going to sports clubs or physical-education training wear their athletic uniform beneath the regulation white jumper and pants, or "white works." Intercollegiate athletes are permitted to wear their varsity-letter sweaters on contest days, without their covers.

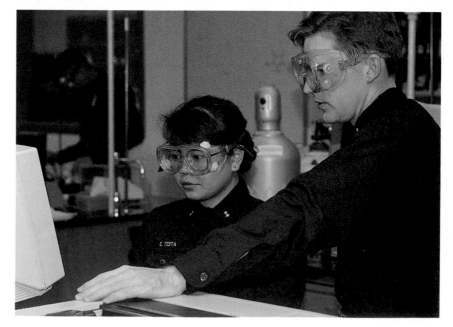

The Naval Academy's academic program is concentrated largely on midshipmen graduating with majors in engineering and the hard sciences, although in recent years about 35 percent of each class has majored in the humanities and social sciences. Upon graduation and commissioning, naval officers will employ their undergraduate classroom and laboratory training in the fleet aboard surface vessels, in nuclear submarines, in the field with marines, and in Navy or Marine Corps aircraft.

Plebes for the most part all take the same academic courses. In the fourth-class year they are required to study calculus, chemistry, leadership, literature, naval science, naval history, government, and computers, plus one elective. These courses are the groundwork for the advanced studies they will pursue as upperclass midshipmen. Upperclassmen also have core subjects, such as electrical engineering, military law, and weapons engineering, that they must complete no matter which major they select. All midshipmen, including plebes, must take a minimum of fifteen credit hours per semester. Many of the upperclassmen often carry a heavier academic load.

The Academy's four-year curriculum is intentionally broad in scope. Bachelor of science degrees are offered in eighteen fields of study: eight in engineering, six in mathematics and the physical sciences, and four in the humanities and social sciences.

Large and small class lectures may cover economics, military leadership, or political science. Laboratory classes in physics, chemistry (such as inorganic and first class independent research), oceanography research and engineering, systems engineering, plus other subjects support classroom instruction with practical exercises. Many of the laboratory problems draw upon situations that midshipmen may encounter in the Fleet.

Each year, a few first-class midshipmen are honored as Trident Scholars, chosen to conduct independent research within their major field of study. Some are selected as Designated Faculty Candidates, while others who have completed their degree requirements may pursue advanced studies at local civilian universities.

Tourists and visitors to the Naval Academy congregate regularly outside Tecumseh Court before the noon meal to watch the brigade form and march into Bancroft Hall. After the brigade commander calls the brigade to attention, the march begins. The brigade commander is the top-ranking first-class midshipman who, with a staff of midshipman officers or "stripers"—so-called because of the gold stripes that they wear on their sleeves—is the 4,200-member brigade's central liaison to the superintendent and commandant. During the winter and inclement weather, all thirty-six companies form on the decks inside Bancroft Hall and head down into King Hall for the noon meal.

At the start of all weekday meals in King Hall (except Friday's evening meal), the brigade commander steps up to the "anchor" or podium in the middle of the dining room and addresses the midshipmen, who are standing at attention by their tables. The announcements are brief: a reminder of the next Forrestal lecture by the Secretary of the Navy or a word about the undefeated wrestling team's match against Army tonight in Alumni Hall. After a blessing from one of the Naval Academy's chaplains, the brigade commander orders, "Brigade, seats!" Forty-two hundred chairs slide at once on the cavernous room's floor as the midshipmen sit down to eat.

"One sunny fall day, while standing watch as a plebe,
I viewed noon meal formation with awe from a lofty perch
in the first wing of Bancroft Hall. As I watched the
brigade commander and his staff march between the
two old cannons guarding Tecumseh Court, I was stunned
when they fired with massive reports, belching fire and
clouds of smoke. I thought the brigade commander
had been assassinated.
Pranksters had, of course, been at work."

Thomas F. Epley, USNA '62

Plebes are constantly reminded of their lowly status as fourth-class midshipmen. Yet, a couple of months after upperclassmen return from summer cruise to start the fall academic semester, some of the traditional tension between plebes and the rest of the brigade eases. Upperclassmen, glad that their plebe days are over, know that the current plebes in their company are future naval officers too. The expressions on the faces of two plebes and their squad members, pictured here, show that awareness.

Midshipmen enjoy participating in harmless horseplay on special occasions, like First-Class Parents' Weekend in September when the "firsties'" parents join their midshipman sons and daughters and their squad members for the noon meal in King Hall.

Midshipmen stay physically fit throughout their Academy days; they must. Through-out their careers in the Navy and Marine Corps they must qualify semiannually on Department of the Navy physical-readiness tests. Midshipmen aiming for commissions as second lieutenants in the Marine Corps work out at the Naval Station across the river from the Academy during "pre-Leatherneck" training sessions, held on Saturday mornings, under the direction of a Marine Corps sergeant major assigned to the Academy's staff. "Leatherneck" is the nickname for the summer program that allows some midshipmen to train for an extended period with the Marine Corps.

During the academic year, the physical-education program is designed to develop physical strength, stamina, and flexibility—including the ability to withstand the physical hardships associated with actual combat or combatlike conditions—as well as a spirit of teamwork and competitiveness, and athletic instructional skills. Midshipmen not on varsity teams must participate in any of the thirty intramural sports, which compete at the battalion and company levels.

Intercollegiate athletics at Navy has a long tradition of winning teams and All-American athletes competing in thirty-three sports (twenty-three for men, ten for women). From men's and women's gymnastics to wrestling and track and field, Navy athletes have brought many national-championship trophies back to Annapolis. The 1992 men's heavyweight crew team, for example, again captured the prestigious Ten Eyck Trophy at the International Rowing Association championships, while the women's crew team took the team-point trophy at Philadelphia's Dad Vail Regatta. The sailing team took the St. David's Lighthouse Trophy in the Newport to Bermuda Yacht Race in 1992. The brigade boxing finals in February is a much-anticipated event. Boxers in the brigade train hard in McDonough Hall for the right to represent their company on either the blue or the gold team.

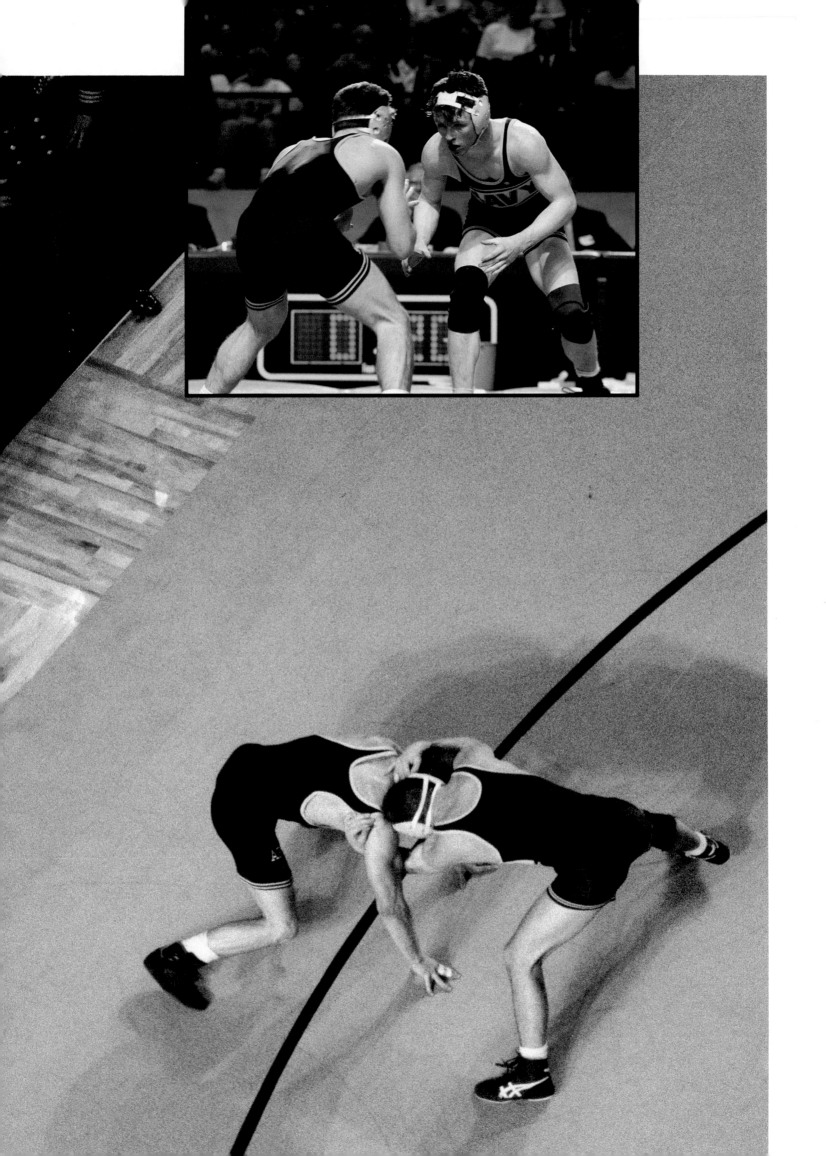

Navy's NCAA Division I-A football schedule is an integral part of life at the Academy during the fall semester. The midshipmen's "march on" to the field at the Navy–Marine Corps Memorial Stadium is not the only tradition peculiar to Navy football. Bill the Goat, Navy's mascot, is paraded, sometimes resisting, along the sidelines by the midshipmen who watch after him. A goat has been the Naval Academy's official mascot since 1904. Plebes assemble in the end zone each time Navy scores and do push-ups for every point the team has totaled. During half time, the award-winning U.S. Naval Academy Drum and Bugle Corps performs. The D&B also plays for every parade, as well as for all of the noon-meal formations in Tecumseh Court.

"As soon as I visited the Naval Academy, I knew this was where I wanted to go to achieve my goals, both scholastically and athletically. Once I made the decision I never looked back, nor have I ever regretted making the choice. As I observe other classmates, I note their leadership positions in private industry, government, and the military. I am confident that a great deal of their success comes from the qualities garnered from experience at the Academy."

Roger Staubach, Chairman and CEO,
The Staubach Company, USNA '65

Navy's cheerleaders are all midshipmen, and theirs is the important job of leading the brigade's cheering of the football team.

Win or lose, the midshipmen happily attend postgame tailgate and tent parties in the stadium parking lot. Although these are a regular feature of Navy football, the "tailgaters" that take place during Homecoming Weekend are special events, allowing the many alumni returning to the Naval Academy to renew old acquaintances and celebrate along with the midshipmen.

The Army-Navy football game is one of the most famous college football classics in the United States. The 103-year-old contest, usually played in Philadelphia, is the season finale for both academies. The entire Corps of Cadets from the U.S. Military Academy at West Point and the Brigade of Midshipmen attend the game, marching into Veterans Stadium well before game time to rouse team spirit and tease the opposing side with an assortment of pranks. The rivalry is so intense that each side will try to kidnap the other team's mascot, and Bill the Goat receives special safeguarding from his midshipman caretakers during the last couple of weeks before the game.

In 1991 Navy's football team made up for a winless schedule with a commanding 24-3 victory over Army. The midshipmen celebrated as if the brigade had won a strategic military campaign. For Navy's midshipmen and Army's cadets, the Army-Navy game is the only one that counts toward a winning football season.

"*The most fun I had as a plebe happened at a regular pep rally one Friday night during football season. For some reason a large group of us suddenly bolted from T-Court, sprinted across the Yard, and headed out the Main Gate and up Maryland Avenue. We ended up running down Main Street to Market Square, where we continued with the pep rally. It was an unexpected and exhilarating taste of freedom for a plebe, and though short, it helped me to get through that first rough semester.*"

Anthony F. Chiffolo, USNA '81

The routines of brigade life exist in public view as well as privately within Bancroft Hall. Visitors enter the dormitory's rotunda daily and gaze into the Naval Academy's main office, staffed twenty-four hours a day by midshipmen of all classes. The telephones they cover are the only phone lines that outsiders can use to contact midshipmen. There are pay phones that mids can use to call out, and some first-class stripers, team captains, and club presidents have telephones in their rooms for company, battalion, brigade, team, or club business.

At 6:00 P.M. the evening watch inspection takes place in the rotunda of Bancroft Hall. The Officer of the Watch, a senior-ranking midshipman, inspects all of the midshipmen assigned watch duty for that evening and the next day. Then they are dismissed and proceed to their posts to start their duty.

All plebes are required to work in teams to create bulletin-board displays within their company's living areas during Plebe Summer and the academic year. These displays are generally professional in nature, depicting special Naval Academy events like Commissioning Week or the Army-Navy game or having naval-service themes such as Marine Corps aviation, submarine warfare, and Operation Desert Storm. But plebes will often take advantage of this occasion to compensate for the pressures of plebe year by gently poking fun at their upperclassmen. Collages of photographs with explanatory headings are the easiest for most time-pressured plebes to arrange, although midshipmen with artistic talent will often paint or sketch some elaborate scenes. These bulletin-board projects teach the plebes to work together toward a common goal.

The weather in Annapolis is often dreary between January and March. Mids call this time of year the Dark Ages. Two midshipmen, pictured here, leave Bancroft Hall and head for class on a foggy February morning. The Dark Ages traditionally end with spring break.

Tecumseh, the Indian figurehead that faces Bancroft Hall and Tecumseh Court, is actually a bronze statue of Tamanend, a peaceful Delaware chief, but midshipmen long ago nicknamed the statue Tecumseh after the war-loving Shawnee chieftain who lived in the late eighteenth and early nineteenth centuries. This figurehead has been at the Academy since 1866. Tecumseh is frequently called the "god of 2.0," which is the minimum passing grade-point average, and some midshipmen toss pennies at Tecumseh en route to their exams for good luck, trying to get the coins into his quiver. Midshipmen paint Tecumseh several times during the year to commemorate special events like Plebe Summer Parents' Weekend, the Army-Navy football game, Homecoming, Halloween, and Commissioning Week.

Midshipmen are encouraged to attend religious services and participate in associated religious activities. The Academy's Main Chapel is the site of Catholic and Protestant services on Sundays, and these are open to the public. Jewish midshipmen attend Friday or Saturday Sabbath prayer in Mitscher Hall. Mids take an active role in these services, reading the lessons, helping the chaplains, serving as ushers, and singing in the choirs.

First-class midshipmen schedule the Main Chapel months ahead of time if they want to be married right after graduation. The military weddings, famous for the newlyweds' kissing under the arch of swords raised by the groom's sword bearers, start almost the moment the new ensigns and second lieutenants are commissioned and continue at the Main Chapel, one after another, for a couple of days. Academy chaplains tell the story of the best man who, late for the wedding and rushing to put on his dress white uniform, ran to the altar during the ceremony and found himself in the middle of the wrong wedding party.

Midshipmen have a wide range of extracurricular activities to choose from. The more than seventy recreational, professional, musical, academic, religious, and community-social clubs and groups help mids balance tough academic and institutional demands with personal interests that are also rewarding.

The brigade's nationally acclaimed Silent Precision Drill Team and the Naval Academy's cheerleaders focus on keeping brigade support high during the year. Midshipmen with musical talents can join the Trident Brass and also the Men's and Women's Glee Clubs. Members of the Glee Club perform Broadway hit shows like *Cabaret* for the general public, as well as travel around the country during vacation periods to publicize the Naval Academy. The athletic groups, like the karate and bicycle clubs, give exhibitions or compete with clubs from other schools. Religious groups like the Officers' Christian Fellowship may sponsor concerts or retreats for the midshipmen. Mids who enjoy community-social activities may spend time on the air with WRNV Radio or may participate in Big Brother–Big Sister events, such as Adopt-a-Grandparent and the USNA School Partnerships program, in which midshipmen tutor Annapolis-area elementary-school children. Midshipmen who can speak foreign languages act as escorts at the annual International Ball, and other midshipmen interested in professional areas work together on the Foreign Affairs Conference or in the Airborne Training Unit, among other professionally oriented groups.

Formal parades are scheduled approximately four times each semester. The late-afternoon ceremony, open to the public, is a popular event for Academy followers. Guests typically include former Academy superintendents, Navy and Marine Corps dignitaries, the brigade's staff of company and battalion officers (active-duty Navy and Marine Corps officers), academic deans, and state and U.S. legislators. At each parade, the superintendent's special guest reviews the brigade as it passes before the reviewing stand.

Parade day is both the pleasure and curse of midshipmen. They admit to its monotony as well as its traditional grandeur. Mids start dressing around 3:10 P.M. in their rooms, and the color guard—the bearers of the flags of the United States, U.S. Navy, U.S. Marine Corps, and Naval Academy—polishes its brass flag bearers. The brigade finally assembles in Tecumseh Court at approximately 3:25 P.M., buttoning and straightening the tight collars of their parade uniforms at the very last minute. After the brigade commander orders, "Draw swords!" thirty-six companies follow the brigade staff down Stribling Walk in front of the Main Chapel on their way to Worden Field. When all of the midshipmen are finally standing at attention on the field, the brigade demonstrates the manual of arms, perfected after long hours of practice. Then the colors are presented, the cannons fire their salute, and finally the brigade passes in review before the superintendent, the commandant, and the rest of the reviewing party.

"For Homecoming '91, everyone in 23rd
Company bought a pair of 'Groucho' glasses,
cut off the noses and moustaches, and wrapped
the bridges of the frames with white tape.
As we marched onto Worden Field, we put our
'geekers' on. The look in those grads' eyes when
they saw a whole company pass in review
with those 'geekers' on was worth getting
put in hack that weekend!"

A. W. Ellermann, USNA '92

Each company is graded on its marching abilities and on the precision of its manual of arms. These grades are factored in with many others collected during the year—such as the success of the company's intramural athletic teams and the grades of the company's midshipmen—to determine which company is the best of the thirty-six. This company is awarded the Color-Company Flag at the Color Parade during Commissioning Week. Despite their complaints about marching in parades, mids enjoy winning the Color Competition because the winning company receives extra privileges for a year.

"I will always remember one formal parade, in which a youngster passed out. As he fell forward, he stabbed a second class in the leg with his bayonet. It drew blood, and the second class would never march anywhere but the back ranks thereafter."

Mark Wm. Stewart, USNA '92

In late January or early February each year, the first classmen choose the specific Navy or Marine Corps duty billet to which they will report after they are commissioned in May. These billets represent the start of each midshipman's career as a junior officer.

Service Selection, as the choosing of billets is known, is as significant to each midshipman as graduation. In fact, many mids will say that Service Selection Day is the purpose of their entire tour at the Naval Academy.

Service Selection starts with the first classmen lining up, according to their Order of Merit, or class ranking, outside the commandant's conference room. A midshipman's Order of Merit is a cumulative, weighted measure of his or her academics, military performance, conduct, physical fitness tests, summer assignments, and professional exams. Virtually everything a midshipman does is closely evaluated by a midshipman's upperclassmen, training officers, company officers, and professors, and class rankings are calculated at the end of every semester. The Order of Merit that is announced just before Service Selection is all-important because it determines who will get his or her first choice of assignments and who may have to settle for second or third choices.

As they approach the conference room, the midshipmen can see on a large television display how many billets are remaining in each major warfare specialty, or "community." Inside, midshipmen announce their selection and learn their fate.

Many midshipmen choose Surface Warfare, the largest community, and are assigned to one of the Fleet's surface vessels. These midshipmen are allowed to select their first ship. Many try to get one of the few billets on the Navy's newest cruisers or destroyers, but other midshipmen opt for spots on an aircraft carrier, amphibious ship, or support vessel. Whichever ship they happen to select, the midshipmen know that as new ensigns they will serve first as division officers, leading between ten and fifty enlisted personnel. This first tour of duty will last some thirty months. Service Selection is the only time they can select the kind of surface-warfare ship on which they will serve.

By the time of Service Selection, those midshipmen who select a spot within the submarine community have already been through an intense series of acceptance interviews and tests. After graduation, these officers will attend nuclear propulsion school, then spend time operating a nuclear plant at one of the Navy's submarine "prototypes,"

next complete Navy Submarine School, and finally report for their first tour of duty aboard an attack or ballistic-missile submarine. Every midshipman who selects the submarine community receives a bonus check for $4,000, as do those mids who choose surface nuclear, who are also prescreened before Service Selection.

Among the most highly prized billets are those for Navy and Marine Corps pilots. Pilot aspirants will complete approximately two years of flight training leading to slots in jet fighters or bombers, helicopters, or patrol, warning-system, or other aircraft.

Midshipmen who want to fly but whose eyesight does not meet the stringent pilot standards choose to become Naval Flight Officers, called NFOs, and will serve as bombardiers, navigators, radar and electronic-intercept officers, and specialists in anti-submarine-warfare systems. Marine Corps NFOs will serve in air command-and-control and antiair-warfare roles. Both the Navy and the Marine Corps also have slots for aviation maintenance and aviation supply. Pilot, NFO, and other aviation selectees are issued the traditional leather flight jackets and aviator sunglasses at Service Selection.

Midshipmen who select Special Warfare—Navy SEALs will attend Basic Underwater Demolition/SEAL school in Coronado, California, right after graduation.

Billets in the Navy's General Unrestricted Line (GURL) are open to all female midshipmen, as well as male midshipmen who are not physically qualified (NPQ) to choose surface warfare, submarines, aviation, or Marine Corps. Assignments can include intelligence, ship duty, shore station, space and electronic warfare, and integrated underseas surveillance systems. The Restricted Line, for NPQ women and men, offers assignments in intelligence, cryptology, geophysics, medicine, engineering, oceanography, and public affairs, among others.

Up to one-sixth of any class at the Naval Academy may choose to enter the Marine Corps. For the Class of 1993, for example, that meant that there were 175 Marine Corps billets, including 15 for women. Upon graduation, new second lieutenants attend the twenty-six-week Basic School for officers in Quantico, Virginia, to study the basics of land warfare, then proceed to advanced training. Each Marine Corps officer will earn an MOS, a military occupational specialty, in fields such as infantry, armor, artillery, logistics, engineering, data processing, and communications.

Besides entering the GURL, female midshipmen may select billets as pilots or NFOs or as surface-warfare officers. However, their assignments are limited to non-combat roles. And female midshipmen who select the Marine Corps can be assigned to all career fields available to male officers except ones that might place them in combat. Recent Policy changes initiated by the Department of Defense may soon lead to combat billets for Navy women pilots and NFOs, female naval officers assigned to combat ships in the Fleet, and women Marine Corps officers leading marines in direct ground-warfare situations.

A select number of midshipmen are allowed to pursue advanced degrees after graduation before beginning their service training. These midshipmen are known as Civilian University Immediate Scholars and may study at MIT, Penn State, Oxford University, or a number of other schools. Other midshipmen qualify as candidates for the Olmstead Foundation Scholars Program or the Navy and Marine Corps Burke Programs, which provide scholarships for advanced studies to be pursued after officers have completed their first tours of duty, about five years after graduation.

Midshipmen are regularly seen walking through the streets of Annapolis during their "liberty," periods when they are authorized to leave the Yard. Plebes must be in uniform virtually all the time at the Academy, including during town liberty on Saturday from 12:15 P.M. until midnight. During Yard liberty, though, plebes may wear regulation Naval Academy athletic gear as a substitute uniform. The only time plebes can wear civilian clothes is when they are home for holidays or when they are visiting their Plebe Sponsor Program families in the surrounding Annapolis area. First-class midshipmen have the most privileges because of their rank. They may wear civilian clothes when they start "Cinderella liberty" after their last military obligation of the day, Monday through Thursday, and must return by midnight. Their weekend liberty starts on Friday after their final military obligation and ends at 7:00 P.M. on Sunday.

III

SUMMER TRAINING

*"Taking command of an infantry platoon in Korea
and each succeeding command thereafter convinced me
that attending the Naval Academy had been the right decision."*

Colonel James W. Hammond, Jr.,

USMC (Ret.), USNA '51

The midshipmen's summer schedules are deliberately planned to give them direct experience in the naval services. Third-class summer, for midshipmen beginning their "youngster" year, includes sailing/seamanship and small-unit-level/leadership training and experience. First, mids take a four-week "cruise" either on a sailboat traveling to New England or the Bahamas, or on an Academy Yard Patrol "YP" craft that tours along the eastern seaboard and makes stops at Newport News, Norfolk, Charleston, Annapolis, and New York. In the YPs, midshipmen apply classroom training in navigation and shiphandling. Next, third-class midshipmen spend four weeks at the U.S. Marine Corps base in Quantico, Virginia, for Midshipman Leadership Training (MLT): three at Marine Officer Candidate School (OCS) and one at The Basic School (TBS). Training at OCS is for the purpose of practicing small-unit-leadership techniques. Midshipmen engage in field exercises and small-unit tactical problems designed to foster teamwork and leadership skills at the small-unit level. The fourth and final week at The Basic School is uniquely Marine Corps in experience. Training includes fire-support-coordination exercises, patrolling, military operations on urban terrain (MOUT), and orientation to tracked vehicles and helicopters. Together, these experiences will help them decide whether they would want to choose the Marine Corps at Service Selection.

Before their junior or second-class year starts, second-class midshipmen are introduced to the major branches of the Navy during a two-week schedule called Professional Training for Midshipmen, or PROTRAMID.

At Pensacola Naval Air Station in Florida they learn about naval aviation, practicing emergency procedures and sea- and land-survival techniques and flying in either T-57 helicopters or T-34 turboprop aircraft. At Kings Bay, Georgia, and Orlando, Florida, second-class midshipmen undertake "submariner" training, practice maneuvering the submarine simulators, and make their first trips in nuclear-powered submarines. When that is over, they sail for four to six weeks on Navy ships and submarines across the globe, working essentially as enlisted petty officers to gain direct knowledge of shipboard life and the essential relationships between naval officers and enlisted personnel.

Once a midshipman begins his or her second-class year, he or she cannot resign from the Academy without incurring an enlisted military obligation to the Navy or Marine Corps.

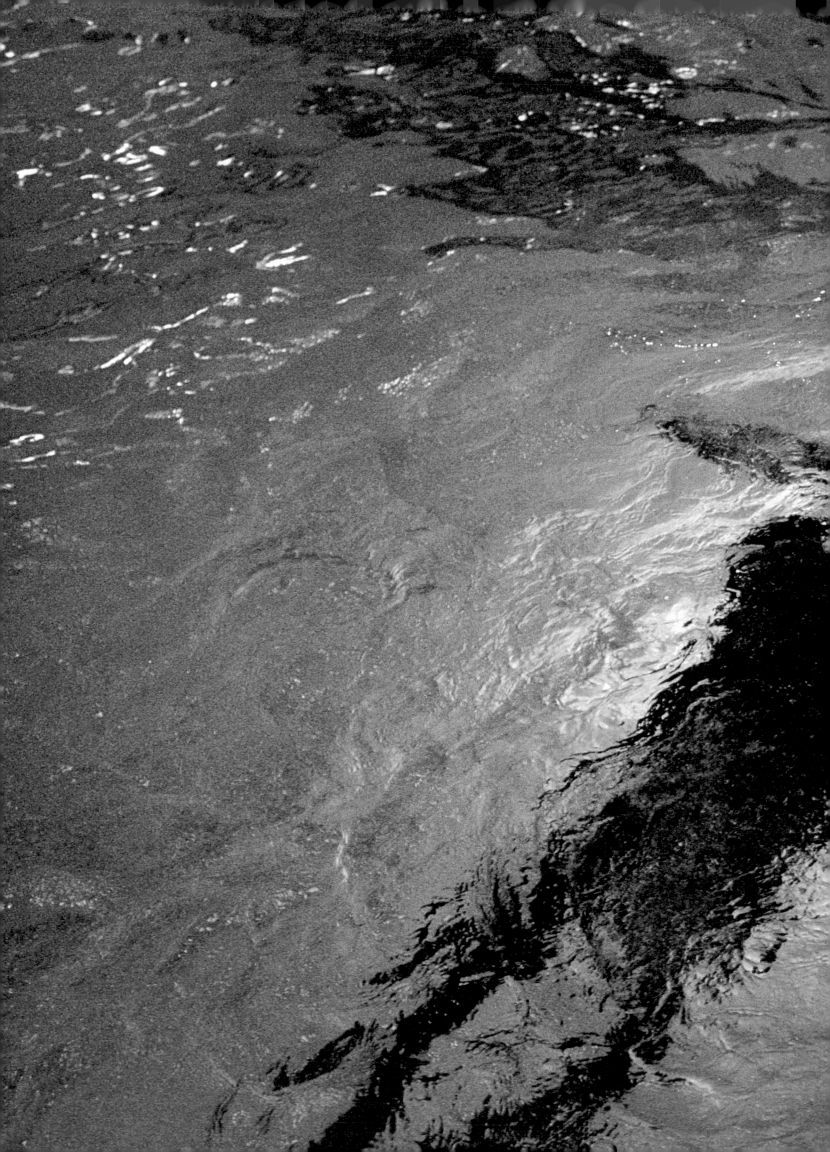

During first-class summer, mids apply their leadership skills in the Fleet, with the Marine Corps, and at the Academy. Some first-class midshipmen join Navy or Marine Corps operational units aboard ships in the Mediterranean, Atlantic, and Pacific and work side-by-side with junior-officer "running-mates." Their daily schedule imitates a junior officer's actual life and duties at sea. Later on, some "firsties" also may attend Marine Corps Leatherneck training at Quantico and learn critical troop-leading and ground-combat skills that will serve them upon commissioning as second lieutenants for those who will choose the Marine Corps at Service Selection in January. Others may also travel for one month on the YPs, serving as instructors for the second-class midshipmen as well as receiving training in boat maneuvers, radio communication, and flag signaling, plus duty-standing instruction while in port. Other first classmen may qualify to serve with foreign navies as part of a foreign-exchange program.

Finally, a select contingent of first- and second-class midshipmen serve as platoon and company commanders and squad leaders for Plebe Summer. They are the first examples of leadership that plebes will observe and develop under during that initial intense period of Naval Academy indoctrination.

"Of the many lessons I learned as a Naval Academy midshipman the most lasting is perseverance—the ability to 'hang in there.' The Academy taught me how to hang on when battered by tough academics, how to force myself to perform well through disappointment and personal tragedy, and how to rise above self-interest and self-pity. Above all, how to accomplish the mission and to do exactly what was expected of me and having done so, to be happy only with the personal satisfaction that comes from doing your duty."

Colonel John W. Ripley, USMC (Ret.), USNA '62

IV

[C]OMMISSIONING WEEK

*"The Naval Academy provided me the opportunity
for a career of service to our Navy and nation. Little did I know
when we took the oath in Memorial Hall how important that and the
traditions of the Academy would be to my future life.
I came as a student with an open mind.
I departed with the desire to command at sea."*

Admiral Frank B. Kelso II, USN,
Chief of Naval Operations, USNA '56

Commissioning Week in May is an assembly of traditional events that symbolize the midshipmen's rites of passage, starting with the closing of plebe year and finishing with the commissioning ceremony.

The Plebe Recognition Ceremony marks the end of plebe year for fourth-class mids and occurs on the first afternoon of Commissioning Week. In the morning the preparations begin when third classmen smear two hundred pounds of lard all over the tree-shaded, twenty-one-foot Herndon monument. At mid-afternoon hundreds of visitors surround the monument to watch the plebes build a human pyramid and scale the obelisk to retrieve a white dixie cup hat fastened at the peak and replace it with an upperclassman's cover.

First, cannons fire and send the charging herd of plebes in athletic gear from Tecumseh Court to Herndon. They throw T-shirts and sneakers against it to wipe off the lard, at the same time building their human wall. The real objective, of course, is for the whole class to work together, relying on the class spirit and sense of teamwork developed over plebe year. Plebes and spectators cheer when the human pyramid rises and groan when it falls apart. The fastest Herndon climb to date was by the Class of 1969, which needed only 1 minute, 30 seconds to scale the monument; most since 1962 have averaged between one and three hours. When the climb is finished, plebes are officially no longer plebes but fourth classmen.

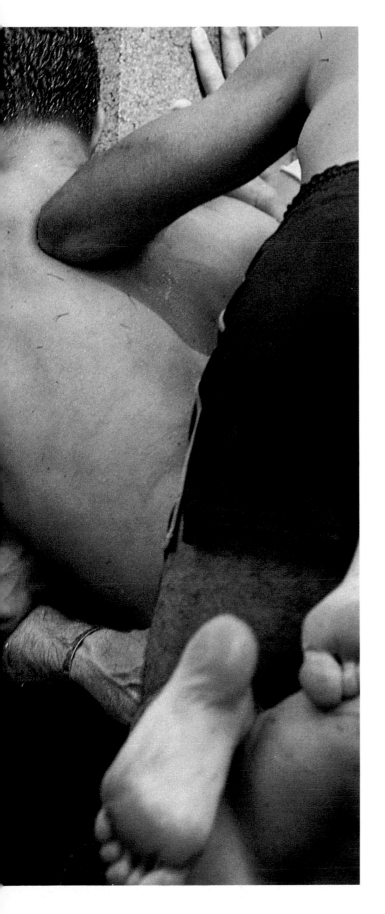

Academy legend is that the midshipman who reaches Herndon's summit and switches the covers will be the first member of the class to become an admiral. The member of the Class of 1995 who made the transfer during 1992's Commissioning Week was a Navy SEAL before he was appointed to the Naval Academy.

Commissioning Week's Dedication and Color Parades are the final ones first-class midshipmen will ever have to march in at the Naval Academy. The soon-to-graduate seniors are ecstatic about that, while the rest of the brigade is jealous. By the time spring arrives in Annapolis, so does its stifling humidity. When the sun shines on parade days, midshipmen prepare to sweat uncomfortably under their heavy wool parade uniforms as they stand at tight attention on Worden Field before Academy officials, dignitaries, and the public.

The Dedication Parade is the first one of Commissioning Week and begins its official festivities, and the brigade is led in review by the stripers who were in charge during the previous fall semester. This parade honors the Academy's faculty members, particularly those who are retiring that year. The Color Parade, led by the spring semester's stripers, occurs on the day before graduation and honors the company that has placed first in the Color Competition. During this parade the Color Company Flag is transferred to the new color company's guidon, or company flag.

Traditionally, when the Color Parade is over, all of the firsties go running for the closest body of water, setting aside their rifles and swords, and jump in, still dressed in their parade uniforms. This marks the end of their duties as midshipmen.

The premier social event of Commissioning Week is the Second-Class Ring Dance. Each midshipman class has designed its own class ring since 1869. Midshipmen receive their rings during the spring semester of their second-class year but are not supposed to wear them until the night of the Ring Dance, although many do wear them secretly.

For the Ring Dance, second classmen dress in their formal uniforms, and their dates wear formal gowns or tuxedos. A midshipman's date wears his ring on a blue ribbon around her neck (or on a wrist chain for the male dates of female midshipmen). The festivities begin with a candlelight dinner in King Hall. Afterward the second classmen and their dates proceed to the dance, which is held, weather permitting, outside around the fountain on Radford Terrace, which is between the academic buildings, and along Stribling Walk.

Sometime during the dance, the date dips the ring into a binnacle containing water from the seven seas. This represents the worldwide travels soon to come for that midshipman as a Navy or Marine Corps officer. Next, the couple steps into a large likeness of the class ring, where the actual ring is slid onto the midshipman's finger and the couple kisses to complete the ceremony.

Graduation is the final event of Commissioning Week. The atmosphere is typical of that of any university commencement, yet graduation from the Academy is also distinctive.

Soon after parents and guests are seated in Navy–Marine Corps Memorial Stadium, the graduating midshipmen walk onto the field in their dress white uniforms. The honors graduates come in first, then the rest of the class marches in by companies.

Several exciting things happen at an Academy graduation. The first one, which occurs early in the schedule, is the "fly over" by the Navy's famous Blue Angels flight demonstration team. Right on schedule, the six McDonnell Douglas F/A-18 Hornet jets streak over the stadium, and the graduating mids raise their fists high in a salute. Earlier in Commissioning Week the Blue Angels present a full aerial show, and thousands of people come to the Academy just to watch the Blue Angels perform their precise airborne acrobatics over the Severn River.

The President of the United States addresses the graduating class every third year; on the off years, the Vice President or a senior U.S. military commander, like the Chairman of the Joint Chiefs of Staff, will send the new junior officers off to their first billet with an uplifting speech.

In 1991 General H. Norman Schwartzkopf, U.S. Army, the Commander of Allied Forces during Operation Desert Storm, gave the Class of 1991 and everyone in the stadium an impressive address and then awarded the midshipmen their diplomas.

"The food is fair. The living accommodations are Spartan.
A weekday, external social life is nonexistent. But the people are
unforgettable, and the career options are impossible to beat."

Christopher A. Eckerle, USNA '92

It is tradition at Navy graduation for families and guests to cheer loudly when their midshipman is called up to receive his or her diploma from the guest speaker and the Superintendent of the Naval Academy. For the mids, this is a moment of uninhibited joy. They dance and strut back down the ramp to join their classmates while they look for their clan up in the stadium seats and proudly display the testament to four years of hard work at a tough institution.

After they receive their diplomas, the graduates are ready for the final event, one they have dedicated four years of sacrifice in a demanding environment to achieve: their commissioning. First, the Commandant of the Marine Corps administers the oath of office to those who chose the Marine Corps. Next, the Chief of Naval Operations swears in the Navy's newest junior officers. It is an instantaneous transformation. Ex-midshipmen are officially second lieutenants and ensigns.

The ceremony officially closes with a tradition that started at Navy in 1912. The president of the new class of firsties calls for three cheers "for those about to leave us." Then the president of the just-graduated class orders three cheers "for those we leave behind," after which the new officers exuberantly fling their old midshipman covers into the air, never to be worn again. Their Academy days are over.

While the dignitaries leave the stadium, the field remains full with graduates and their families. Parents, brothers and sisters, fiancées, and others pin Navy ensign boards and Marine Corps second lieutenant gold bars onto the graduates' uniforms. The new firsties, second classmen, and third classmen may also stick around, congratulating the new officers, who by tradition give a silver dollar to the first person to salute them.

As for the covers they tossed away moments before? Those are replaced immediately with crisp new ones for Navy and Marine Corps officers. One significant journey has ended and another is about to start.

ACKNOWLEDGMENTS

This project granted me a special association with the Naval Academy. I am largely indebted for much of its achievement to the generosity, enthusiasm, immense cooperation, and friendship of a number of people, most of whom are connected directly with the U.S. Naval Academy and the naval service.

First, I sincerely want to thank Commander Mike John, the U.S. Naval Academy's Public Affairs Officer, and his outstanding staff. All of them gave considerable time out of their busy days and coordinated my photo schedules, expedited my access to key Academy events, extended good advice and suggestions, and always made me feel a welcome part of their great institution. Besides Commander John, my wholehearted appreciation goes to Noel Milan, Karen Myers, Diane Olmstead, Lieutenant Kelly Merrell, Debbie Carroll, and the rest of the civilian and military public-affairs staff for their enormous help and interest.

I certainly extend that same appreciation to Dave Eckard, Wayne McCrea, Ken Mierzejewski, and Alex Hicks of the U.S. Naval Academy's Photographic Branch, also part of the public-affairs staff. All four men were trusted fellow photographers and, in a short time, became good friends whose thoughtfulness, assistance, and terrific sense of humor helped me produce a lasting book for the Naval Academy family.

My thanks go to Robert Burgard, USNA '61, Vice Admiral William P. Lawrence, USN (Ret.), and others who helped me appreciate the timeless principles and uniqueness of Naval Academy life by reminding me that my photographs should always capture those special moments.

I had the pleasure to meet some fine officers who generously took me inside the corridors of Bancroft Hall, showed me what went on at Pensacola Naval Air Station, and guided me through the Marine Corps base at Quantico. They answered every question I had about the mids and the Academy's ways and made me feel lucky to have known them. Thanks to Ensigns Tom Frosch, Hunter Ware, Dave Hanson, Chris Eckerle, and John Fitzgerald and Lieutenants Mike Genereaux and Greg Adair, U.S. Navy, and Lieutenant Colonel Charles Peterson and Second Lieutenants Scott Kish and Grace Gee, U.S. Marine Corps.

Three midshipmen who provided assistance and interest, for which I am grateful, were Midshipman 1/C Matthew Reimann and Midshipmen 2/C Brad Rosen and Jeremy Jorgenson.

I also want to thank Tom Epley, Anthony Chiffolo, John Cronin, Shannon Becker, Karen White, and the rest of the editorial, production, and marketing staffs at the Naval Institute Press with whom I had the pleasure to work. They were committed to making this project a timeless photographic story of the Naval Academy.

Finally, my very special gratitude to Pam Stewart, my wife, Melody and Martin Gallahan, and Paul Tilley. Each was very generous in understanding my passionate belief in the book and helped in so many ways to make it happen.

TECHNICAL DATA

Cameras	Nikon F3HP
	Nikon FE2
Film	Kodachrome 64
	Kodachrome 200
	Ektachrome 100 Plus
	Ektachrome 160T
	Fujichrome 400
Lenses	Nikkor 16mm f/2.8
	Nikkor 24mm f/2.8
	Nikkor 35mm f/1.4
	Nikkor 85mm f/2
	Nikkor 105mm f/2.5
	Nikkor 180mm AF f/2.8
	Nikkor 300mm AF f/2.8
Flash	Nikon SB-16B Speedlight

ABOUT THE AUTHOR

Robert Stewart has been a freelance journalist and photojournalist for eleven years. In 1988 he published *Rowing The Experience*, an all-color photo-documentary on the sport of rowing in the United States, and his photos appear in *The Book of Rowing* (1988). His photographs are also featured in the new book *Brigade Seats! The U.S. Naval Academy Cookbook* (Naval Institute Press, 1993). As a journalist for magazines and newspapers, his assignments have included hard news, national investigative reporting, profiles, and special-section pieces for various publications, including *The New York Times*. He lives in New Jersey with his family.

THE NAVAL INSTITUTE PRESS

THE BRIGADE IN REVIEW
A Year at the U.S. Naval Academy

Designed by Karen L. White

Set in Centaur and Castellar on a Macintosh IIci
and output by Baltimore Color Plate
Baltimore, Maryland

Printed on 80-lb. Repap Lithofect enamel
by The John D. Lucas Printing Company
Baltimore, Maryland

Bound in ICG Kennett
by American Trade Bindery, Inc.
Baltimore, Maryland